"THE INTERIOR LIGHT"
Activate your greatness

By:
Alessio David Ricioppo Parra

About the author:

Alessio David Ricioppo Parra, born on date 21st September 1988 in Genoa, with double citizenship (Spanish and Italian) is an advanced yogi, who started to practice yoga at the age of 16 and that loves to help people to be happier, to grow in a better version of themselves and achieving their dreams.

copyright ©
Year of release - 2017
Alessio David Ricioppo Parra
THE INTERIOR LIGHT
Activate your greatness

ISBN 978-0-244-60726-5
Published thanks to: lulu.com
All rights reserved

Official website: theinteriorlight.wordpress.com
Business email: theinteriorlight@gmail.com

Legal notices:

ACKNOWLEDGEMENTS

"First of all, I would like to thank my wonderful father for always being present for me and for having taught me yoga. I would also like to thank all my dear ones – each of you is a true gift in my life. I would also like to thank the people who used to be close to me and with whom I shared wonderful moments, even if now we are no longer part of each other life. Thanks to each of you, I learned precious life lessons that made me in the person that I am today and I am continually improving in a better version of myself."

SUMMARY

INTRODUCTION

Thousands of years ago, Lao Tzu wisely said: *"A journey of a thousand miles begins with a single step"*. Our journey together starts here and now, and the first step is telling to you, my readers, how my interest in yoga started. Yoga is the greatest gift and the most authentic joy in my life. There was always a special connection between us. One day when I was a baby (I was just 14 days old) and bursted into tears, screaming in pain, my father sang me the mantra "OM"; so after five minutes I stopped crying and fell asleep - and I felt this special connection for the first time. As time passed I started reading books about Yoga: I immediately liked it and began to practice it. My first lesson was when I was 16 years old and in many years of experience, yoga taught me a lot of valuable life lessons. But most importantly, yoga has taught me to love myself and always believe in myself! That's why I love yoga with all my heart. Yoga was, is and will always be an important part of my life. My purpose in life is to help people to grow and achieve their potential. This book is aimed with the purpose to share wisdom and positivity in a variety of topics, and helping you – my readers – to brighten and improve your life in many different areas – achieving a better understanding of yourself and of life, including the business field and even personal relationships. Don't search the light – become the light. A positive light for yourself and for your dear ones. It's about time to start our walk together step by step.

UNIVERSAL LAW OF LIFE – KARMA

According to scientific models, the universe used to be a hot conglomerate of energy until many billions of years ago, when an event called Big Bang happened. Fundamental natural forces started to spawn: electromagnetism, gravity, weak nuclear force, strong nuclear force. Space-time was born, particles emerged as the universe started to expand, stars and galaxies started to appear in the universe. One day in the planetary system around the star called Sun, on this planet, all the ideal conditions were met in order for life to take place, beginning with cellular level life forms to more complicated ones, and continually evolving. Many thousands of years ago, yogis discovered that every living being is under the effect of a universal law, known as "Karma". Karma is a Sanskrit word, it means "action." Karma regulates the flow of life on energetic level – with the currency of your karmic actions, you create with your hands all your life experiences – good and bad, pleasant and unpleasant. Thus every person shapes personally their own destiny with their own thoughts, words and deeds. Karma thus can be regarded as the spiritual equivalent of Newton's law of motion: "*There is an equal but opposite reaction for every action.*" If you put positive energy in the universe, positive energy will be returned back to you. Instead if you put negative power in thought, word or action, that negative energy returns back to you. Karma is often misunderstood and saw merely as a punishing force, but that's not it. Karma is merely present for education purposes - showing that a harmful action is wrong, in order to learn life lessons to people and grow spiritually as individual. A person will only suffer by creating personally the conditions for suffering.

There are 12 known laws of karma.

Law of Karma No. 1 - The Great Law.

"As you sow, so you shall reap"

This is also known as the Law of Cause and Effect. Whatever we put in action in the universe, it is what comes back to us. Our thoughts and actions have consequences – positive or negative, whatever they are immediate or not. If we want peace, love, harmony, prosperity, etc - then we must be ready to act accordingly and be peaceful, loving, harmonious, prosperous etc... Negative energy sent to others, will return back to you 10 times stronger in order to teach you that an harmful action is wrong.

Law of Karma No. 2 – The Law of Creation.

"What we want in life is obtained due to participation."

Life does not just happen, it requires our participation. Since we are one with the universe, both inside and outside, our intentions determine the evolution of all existence. The life that we see around us was created according to the intentions of living beings. What surrounds us, gives us clues to our inner state. We are responsible for making this environment conducive to our desires, therefore be and do what you want to have in your life.

Law of Karma No. 3 – The Law of Humility.

"Refusal to accept what is, will still be what it is."

We must first accept the current circumstances in order to change them. What you refuse to accept will continue for you. If we see an enemy or a person with a character trait, which we consider negative, we ourselves are not focused on a higher level of existence. Focusing on the negative does not change the situation. By focusing attention to make a positive change in your life, you will change your life.

Law of Karma No. 4 - The Law of Growth.

"People either grow together or grow alone. Our spiritual growth is above any circumstances."

Wherever you go, there you are. To grow, we ourself must change - not the people, places and things around us. The only thing that we have control on - is ourselves. The subsequent action or inaction will give either positive or negative circumstances in our life. When we change who and what we are in our heart, our lives will also change.

Law of Karma No. 5 – The Law of Responsibility:

"I'm not who you think I am. You are what you think me to be. Our life is our own business, not of someone else."

When turbulence occurs in your life, an internal storm often occurs. We mirror what surrounds us, and what surrounds us mirror us. This is why this law is also known as the "Law of Mirrors". When someone emphasizes something in you (regardless of whatever it can be a good or a bad label), it means that it is in them, and if you see the same quality in them, it is in you as well. Otherwise it is not in you, but it is in them. This is a powerful truth, because if someone calls you with a bad label and you do not know why they think that then you will realize that it is not you, it is them - and you will not feel the need to prove or convince them otherwise, knowing that they simply can not see it. If we want to change our lives, we must take responsibility for what is in our lives, changing our mood and environment.

Law of karma No. 6. The Law of Communication.

"Everything is connected – big or small. Past, present and future are all connected."

Even if at first glance, what we are doing may seem insignificant – in truth our past, present and future are correlated. Therefore, we must make changes in the steps of our life journey if we want something else. Each step leads to the next step, etc. To complete a task, you must take the first step to the goal. Each step of the process has the same value – they are all equally necessary for the completion of a task.

Law of Karma No. 7 - The Law of Focus.

"You can not focus on two things at once"

It is important to have a "step by step" mentality, focusing on the step of the present moment. As for our spiritual growth, we cannot have negative thoughts or actions, as all attention should be directed towards achievement.

Law of Karma No. 8 – The Law of Giving and Hospitality

"Demonstrating what we learned in practice and our selflessness by true intentions."

What we claim to believe to be true, it must be manifested into our actions. Sometimes in your life you will be called upon to that truth you learned in practice. Selflessness is a virtue only if we are accommodating something other than ourselves. Without a selfless nature, true spiritual growth is nearly impossible.

Law of Karma No. 9 - The Law of "Here and Now"

"Carpe Diem"

You can not go back to the past and change what happened. Looking back with regret and forward pointlessly prevent us to being fully present in the only moment that truly matters - the "here and now". Old thoughts, patterns and dreams prevent you from having new ones, thus denying the possibility to move forward and advance yourself.

Law of Karma No. 10 – The Law of Change

"Everything happens for a reason. History will continue to repeat itself, unless it is changed."

History will continue to repeat itself, until we learn the lesson and thus we make a conscious commitment in directing our positive energy to change our path.

Law of Karma No. 11 – The Law of Patience and Reward

"Rome was not build in one day. The creation of everything of value requires a patient mindset."

Even the longest path starts with a single step. Rewards of lasting value require a patient mindset and hard work. You only fail if you quit. Rewards are not the end result. True, lasting joy comes from knowing what to do in the right expectation of a reward that is well earned.

Law of Karma N° 12 – The Law of Significance and Inspiration:
"The best reward is the one that contributes to the whole"
The value of something is directly linked to the energy and intent you have put into it. Every personal contribution also contributes to the whole. The end result is of little value if it leaves little or no impact on the whole or work to diminish it.

What we think, we become.
It's important to always keep a positive attitude.
Always be grateful, act with love, check your motives, watch your attitude and forgive. Positivity is much stronger than negativity, and you should always look at the positive bright side of a situation and what positive lesson you can learn from it. Negativity can only affect you if you are vibrating at the same energetic frequency, vibrate higher by remaining positive and you will not create any negative karma in that way. Also by acting positively, you will clean the negative karma you might have previously created – this process is known as "karmic cleanse". Instead by acting negative and fearful, not only you create negative

karma but you will also create the required environment of thoughts, pattern and actions that will eventually cause what you fear to happen be attracted in your life in the first place. Fear is only an illusion – so face everything and rise. Life is an echo - if you are acting positively and you are focusing on the present moment, fear cannot exist. This said, we can classify two main categories of karma - individual karma and collective karma. The difference is simple. Individual karma is the one created by a living being, while collective karma is a sum of karma created by a group of living beings. It is interesting to notice that collective karma is the basis of the event called "historical cycles". By observing history, you can notice how certain patterns in human society try to repeat. It is not a coincidence – rather an expression of collective karma seeds created by lot of people over a long period of time that activates periodically due to the appropriate conditions. On a larger scale, this collective karma of all living beings affect the whole universe to the point of having a variable predominant background effect on it. The lowest point is called "kali yuga", in which ignorance and violence are predominant. As the global collective karma improves, universe enters in "dvapara yuga" (in which there is a better average understanding of "space"), then improves in "tetra yuga" (better average understanding of "time") and finally "satya yuga" (highest average positive background and alignment to karma universal law) and then gradually lower again back to kali one step at time. Right now, universe in an ascending phase – the lowest point of kali yuga was touched mostly around Middle Age (an age of extreme ignorance and violence) and we gradually entered some hundreds of years ago in an ascending phase of "dvapara yuga".

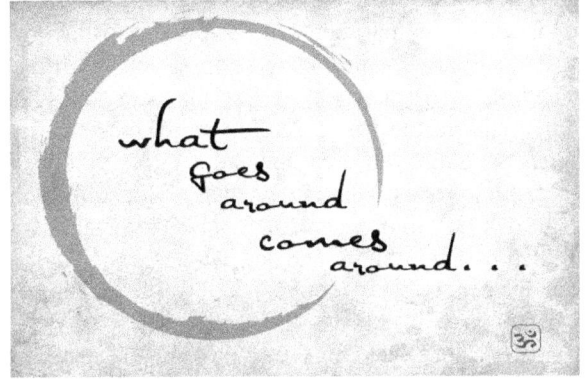

YIN AND YANG

By observing universe, many dualities can be noted: hot and cold, wet and dry, up and down, etc... And usually they tend to be treated by many people as opposites forces that they can not coexist. But if you look impartially at the bigger picture, you will notice something interesting. Let us take for example - "hot" and "cold". In the first case, you might think to fiery flames scorching an area and reducing everything in their path to ashes. In the second case, you might think to the winter environment of Siberia, with massively low temperature, snow and icy wind. At first sight, they have nothing in common. However by looking deeper, you will notice something. In order to define an object "hot", there must be a polar opposite concept - which in this case is "cold". Also the two objects must be able to be compared using a relative scale and in this case the factor used for this purpose is called "temperature". Temperature is expressed by a number that is linked to the amount of heat, and the amount of heat is determined by the vibration and movement on atomic level. "Absolute cold" is the condition in which such atomic vibration and motion is completely stopped. The higher is such vibration and motion and the more heat will be produced with "absolute hot" being the condition in which the vibration is at maximum possible as motion reach light speed – but as now, neither of the two extreme condition has been replicated in a laboratory and they are classified as purely theoretical.

Now let us take our Sun... We can say that Sun can be actually "hot" and "cold". Sun is "hot" when it is compared to a planet like Earth, however there are stars which can produce many more times the heat than Sun itself and in this case Sun would be classified as "cold" compared to them. That is what the concept of Yin Yang express. The dualities are not opposites that they can not coexist, rather they are complementary aspect of the unity of the whole. As such the symbol for yin yang is represented by a circle composed by two sides: half is black, half is white, and in each of them there is a dot of the other color. It is a powerful reminder that for every situation in life, there are always going to be a positive and a negative side – so you should always focus on the positive and what positive lesson you can learn from the situation at hand. After all, love and positivity are the most powerful force of connection, spiritual growth and expansion.

LIFE IS A JOURNEY

In such a fascinating universal context, one day we were born. Each of us is an unique expression of the whole, with limitless potential. Native Americans believed that Earth was the "mother" of us all, thus they treated our planet and other animals with great respect. And they did not claim any ownership on land or seas, seeing themselves as witnesser and a passenger on this planet. Life is a journey and everyone's journey is different. Situations change, people come and go in your life and you learn valuable lessons. It is the refusal to accept the flow of the world that causes misery and suffering. In this individual journey, each of us gets two powerful instruments at disposal: mind and body, two sides of the same coin. Try to observe the difference on how you breath between when you feel nervous and when you feel calm. In the first case each breath will be superficial and fast, in the second each breath will be deeper and last longer. Now, next time that you feel nervous, start to breath deeper, with your abdomen pushing towards outside when you breath in, and returning towards your spine as you breath out – making each breath long. Do for a while and observe how you feel – you will gradually start to feel calmer – that is the proof that mind and body are correlated. Eastern medicine is well aware of this fact and, unlike western medicine, prefers to focus on finding the deeper cause of an illness. For example let's take the illness known as "gout". In western medicine, doctors would usually give a medicine about the inflammations – which is just a temporary relief and the patient will return for more anti-inflammatory later. Oriental medicine will instead address the problem by going deeper, not only giving a temporary relief but by studying the cause and suggesting possibilities to prevent further problems – and in this case, it would be about some changes in the diet of the patient and ensuring the patient drinks more water, therefore reducing the deposit of the substances that create the inflammatory arthritis. Yoga is also a powerful medical tool – there is a brilliant book about this topic, "Yoga as medicine" of Timothy McCall. I suggest you to read it. By looking even deeper, illnesses are caused by disfunctions in the vital energy system that cause in turn the formation of energy blocks. These energy blocks can either affect the body directly like in the case of stress related illnesses (like chronic stomachache or headaches) and/or cause a weakening of the immune system that eventually allows the harmful virus and bacteria to infect the body. In the eastern the existence of vital energy has been known since thousands of years and it has been called with many different names – ki, prana, qi... Many useful techniques has been created to correct these energetic dysfunctions - like pranotherapy/reiki, acupuncture etc... In the western, Reich was able to extrapolate this same vital energy, calling it "orgone", even creating objects that conduct its flow in a "pranotherapy/reiki" way and used them to treat critical patients with outstanding documented results. Vital energy does not just influence the health of the body, it goes much deeper than that. Vital energy has two aspects: one is masculine energy, and the other is feminine energy.

Masculine energy is about logic, breaking barriers, action, survival. Feminine energy is about emotion, connection, healing and nurturing. Everyone of us has both energies inside. By nature most people are stronger in one and weaker in the other during their lifetime. Men tend to be more centered in masculine energy, and women to be more centered in feminine energy. As a result of this, women tend to be driven by emotions and men tend to be driven by logic. Everything that a woman does and says is the result of her emotional state in the present moment, while men tend to be more logical and focused on the goal in life. Having realized and understood this truth, it is possible to achieve mutual understanding, communication without difficulties, and effortless romantic relationships (in which for a sexual polarity to exist, one partner must be centered in masculine core and one partner centered in feminine core - in heterosexual relationships this is usually achieved by a "masculine" man paired with a "feminine" woman). It's important to keep in mind that while you can strengthen the weaker energy by the example of another person, you shouldn't rely on another unbalanced person to restore your personal energy through relationships. In order to be a complete person, you must own your main core while at the same time being aware of the existence of both energies and the timing to use them, as certain life situations might require more one of the two. Another common trait of living beings is the freedom to be ourself, which is a reflection of universal freedom. Every person resents the potential loss or the loss of freedom, and that's why neediness is a natural repulsor in human interactions – by interacting with a needy person, you will fell that your freedom is at risk. True love is freedom. You must love yourself first, that is the prerequisite to create a great lifestyle and relationships. After all, you are the person that you will spend your entire life with. Loving yourself means that you will not tolerate the presence of negative people sticking around in your life, bringing constant drama and trying to put you down the whole time. You should always evaluate the actions of other people - to the ones who appreciate you, give the gift of your presence and to the ones who try to put you down and disrespect you, give the gift of your absence. The purpose of life is to enjoy this journey, making it emotionally compelling to you and to satisfy your deep desire of greatness and growth as a person. Do not put the key of your happiness in someone else pocket, happiness is found within. I love to see people happy and succeeding.

SOCIETY AND SOCIAL CONDITIONING

In ancient times, the first humans started to gather together in tribes to facilitate survival and thus the first societies were born. In ancient society, men were defenders, they protected their families from being eaten and taken away. Men provided for the safety of the family, so their families could trust them so that they would face critical situations and feel protected. To be a mountain means to be a defender. Today, our dear ones rely on us men because they know that we can protect them from dangers and can afford to be vulnerable emotionally and physically. They know that they will not be humiliated. They know that they are always been protected from dangers and troubles. To be a mountain means to provide a life in which they can find love, understanding, emotional security, physical security and acceptance – a real man is a hero for himself and his loved ones. As society evolved, we passed from nomad hunting tribes to a more sedentary life style – with the creation of the first villages, introducing agriculture, cities, trading, money, countries, etc... And thus gradually bringing to our current social structure. The true motive of current society lies actually in two main components: the capitalistic ego-driven system, and the will of the ruler of social communities to control the local group of people of a certain area of jurisdiction. Society is not interested in helping to develop their unique traits of individuals. The rulers of social communities prefer to have a bunch of people that do not question anything, that bring capitalistic profit to the system and to themselves, and that they all think all in a certain model as in this way they are easy to control and manipulate at will. A great representation of this mechanism can be found in the book "1984" written by Orwell. Anyone and anything that touches the "*normality*" defined in this way thus becomes a potential disruptive force of the system. In order to reduce the birth of potential freethinkers, societies tries to brainwash people, using mainly two instruments: education system and media. Starting from childhood, social structure tries to implant ideas about a certain model of life and they normally try to repress their creativity and free-thinking. That is for example the reason why left handed children are often forced to learn to write with the right – as left handed people tend to be on average more creative. Also brainwashed people would subconsciously try to brainwash kids without realizing it. In addition to this mechanism, medias are also powerful complementary tools. They are great in manipulating information in a way that favours current social structure and the proposed model of "*normality*" of the local community.

Typical manipulation techniques of medias are generating fear and generate false needs to follow the scripted model.

Telenews, newspaper and internet are usually the main generator of fear in communities, thus influencing a vast majority of people of the local community to do as the rulers of social structure exactly want. A great mechanism that rulers of social structures love to implement for doing this is an ancient Latin war stratagem: *"Divide et impera"* (= Divide and conquer).

Any organized method that causes such separations is greatly appreciated by the head of social structure. Organized cults that promote hate of other groups. Organized sports that put people one against the other. The overstatement of news regarding members of other communities stealing etc (when there are also local members of the same communities doing that for instance and not getting nearly the same weight) is a subtle try to generate racism – and the reason is simple: by members of different communities interacting, it is easier to see the manipulation plan of social structures as rulers of different social structures might implement certain ideas differently to manipulate people. The whole idea of country is a magnification of *"Divide et impera"* on a larger spread – simply the manipulation happens on a much larger collection of local communities. Look at the Earth: do you see any borders limiting country? No, there are not any. Those borders are imaginary; they are just conventions to favour certain people in their benefits. In truth, we are all world citizens. The generation of false needs applies both in the wish that a certain model is followed blindly, and both in a capitalistic profit. I will make a specific example: tv spots.

Tv spots use an alterated version of a positive yoga technique, called *"affirmations"*. The original yoga technique works like this: by reading every day, in a relaxed receptive status, positive affirmations – said affirmations will enter your subconscious mind. By doing so, they will gradually shape you in the desired positive direction . It does sound familiar, doesn't it? Tv spots alterated this, by creating a negative version.

They put on tv spots by interrupting at the climax point of a show, film etc when the person is more receptive. The volume is increased compared to the regular volume of the film and show to boost the impact. The constant repetition will cause the message to enter the subconscious mind, and create a false need to buy an object the person does not really need. As result, there are going to be many people exposed to the tv spot that will eventually start to buy more and more of the target product, thus benefitting the capitalistic system of society.

Many people fall in the trap of the social manipulation and become like "zombies": they follow blindly the mass and media, live by the model, they don't discover their true gifts and talents, and one day they will die without having truly lived.

Steve Jobs did a wonderful speech at Standford University – an absolute must read and watch. I will quote one part: *"Your time is limited, so don't waste it living someone else's life. Don't be trapped by dogma — which is living with the results of other people's thinking. Don't let the noise of others' opinions drown out your own inner voice. And most important, have the courage to follow your heart and intuition. They somehow already know what you truly want to become. Everything else is secondary."* (Steve Jobs)

You are not responsable for the social conditioning and programming you received, especially when you were a child. However as an adult, you are 100% responsable to fix the situation and take power back and control yourself and your life. Travel as much as possible and interact with people different cultures.

Think with your own head. Observe and meditate. Feel in your heart what you really want. Discover your unique traits, gifts and talents and explore them. Let your positive and weird light shine so brightly and uniquely, that others weirdos will know exactly where to find you.

THE BIG 5 - "O.C.E.A.N"

According to psychological studies, we can note the presence of 5 main traits – also known as "Big Five" (or with the acronym O.C.E.A.N.) - that contribute to the formation of personality in an individual.

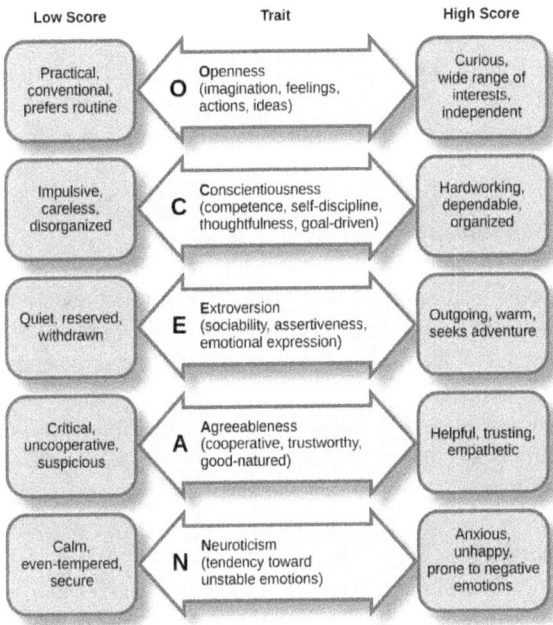

Low Score	Trait	High Score
Practical, conventional, prefers routine	**O** Openness (imagination, feelings, actions, ideas)	Curious, wide range of interests, independent
Impulsive, careless, disorganized	**C** Conscientiousness (competence, self-discipline, thoughtfulness, goal-driven)	Hardworking, dependable, organized
Quiet, reserved, withdrawn	**E** Extroversion (sociability, assertiveness, emotional expression)	Outgoing, warm, seeks adventure
Critical, uncooperative, suspicious	**A** Agreeableness (cooperative, trustworthy, good-natured)	Helpful, trusting, empathetic
Calm, even-tempered, secure	**N** Neuroticism (tendency toward unstable emotions)	Anxious, unhappy, prone to negative emotions

Let us go deeper in each trait.

Openness to experience

This trait refers to the degree of intellectual curiosity, creativity and variety a person has. It is also related to the extent of independency of a person. Persons with high openness/adventurous tend to be more unpredictable, to pursue self-actualization by intense experiences, and they usually appreciate art, adventure, emotions, creative ideas and variety of experiences. Low openness/routinary tend to favour routine, perseverance, and they are data-driven – in the most extreme cases a low openness is dogmatic and closed-minded.

Conscientiousness

An organized/efficient personality tend to be focused on self-discipline, act dutifully, aim for achievement and prefer plans and preparation over spontaneous behaviour – at his peak, to the point of stubbornness and obsession. A more careless-easy going personality is associated with flexibility and spontaneity, however at his peak it can appear as sloppy and lacking reliability.

Extroversion

An outgoging/extrovert personality tend to be energized by external simulation (company of others, attention seeking behaviour, talkativeness). A more introverted/reserved person tend to be energized more by having some alone time and by internal stimulation – such type of personality might be perceived as aloof or self-absorbed.

Agreeableness

A more friendly personality is more compassionate and cooperative, at its peak can be naive or submissive. A more challenging personality is more suspicious and antagonistic towards others – and often very competitive, which can be perceived as argumentative or untrustworthy.

Neuroticism

Nervous personality is emotionally reactive and it experiences negative emotions easier and for an extended period of time – tending to be emotionally unstable, pessimistic and often in bad mood. Secure personality is emotionally stable, less upset and less reactive – tending to be calm, optimistic and free from negative feelings.

People who do not show any clear tendency towards specific areas on the 5 traits can be considered adaptable, moderate personalities – in some occasion they can be perceived as unprincipled, inscrutable and calculating.

Children tend to have a more unstable personality.
In childhood, the feminine core of a woman tend to pre-program women to pursue the power of a main male figure: when they are kids that person is their father, when they become adult the main male figure will become their romantic partner. That is why women are more attracted to men who have a "take it or leave it" attitude (in other words "being happy, regardless if she is with him or she is not and she chooses someone

else") and let women pursue them – smart men let women come and go as they feel comfortable. Chasing is a feminine trait, so women should do the majority of chasing and talking in dating scene, with the man doing (if necessary) an initial effort in the beginning of dating until her attraction starts to grow enough for her to start pursuing or else the attraction by her part will drop.

Returning to the Big 5, it is important to notice that there is a range between the two points of each trait and while the personality become more stable at reaching adulthood, an individual personality might change over time – thanks to life experiences and lessons. Each person might have by nature a different set of affinities in each of the 5 traits, but they are not set in stone. So for example a person with an affinity to a more "nervous personality" in neuroticism can learn to become secure, even if more work would be needed compared to one with a natural affinity to a secure personality in the same trait.

COMMUNICATION

Communication is composed by 3 parts:
-Words
-Tone of voice
-Body language

Words work like a link to a visual image or concept.
When you talk, concepts and visual image are expressed in the form of words of the target language. At the same time, by reading or listening a word, associated concept and visual image will come to mind – let us say for example "pink elephant": as you red it, a pink elephant comes to your mind.
However words are just part of a communication.
And to be more precise, just the tip of the iceberg.
93% of communication is actually not verbal (tone of voice and body language). In order to be fully congruent all of the 3 parts of a message should be consistent with each other.

Body language tips
-A genuine smile will encompass the whole face, including eyes. A fake smile will usually only involve lips.
-Open body language (open legs, open arms, not putting object as barriers, open palms..) tend to indicate an open mindset towards the other person and make the other person feel welcome. Mirroring the body language of another is also a sign of agreement with that person.
-Close body language (folded legs, folded arms, putting objects between ourselves and the other person,

closing eyes when talking to someone, etc...) tend to indicate a signal of shielding, disagreement and mental closure towards the other person.

-Feet position indicates the focus of attention, and if they are insistently pointed to an exit/opposite direction they might signal the desire of that person to go away.

-Eyes position indicates the channel of the nervous system used when a person talks. Typically: *looking down is related to emotion, looking up to visual, looking left to construct images and looking right to memory.* Therefore if a person looks up and left is a signal of visual construction of an idea, while looking up and right is a signal of a visual remembering. In rarer case people might use a different correlation in channels, but asking specific questions that cause a specific reaction will give you the confirmation.

-Women tend to send non-verbal clues when they feel attraction and they are open to flirting with a combination of various signals, including: *open body language, playing with their hair, looking down when you look at her, eyes widening, pupil growing, blushing, pigeon toes, shoulder shrouds, playfulness, sudden freezes while talking, exposing neck, exposing wrists, forehead bow, head tilting, sideways glance over raised shoulders, smiling, laughing and giggling, changing in voice to mirror the target of interest, touching, playing nervously with a necklace/bracelet/etc...* When several signals like these are present in an interaction, it's safe to assume the girl is interested. When a woman feels ready to be kissed, she will non-verbally communicate it by:

1) looking back at the lips of the target of interest as

the target is very close to her and slowly look her in the eyes, lips, and back to her eyes for a few second interval or 2) she will "triangulate" by looking at the lips of the target of interest, which will trigger her to look down (emotional response) then suddenly she will looks somewhere else and restarts the "triangulation" circle.

-A wide stance with foot more apart from each other indicates higher power and confidence. Especially combined with open body language and looking another person in the eyes.

The importance of distance in communication

During communication in person, it is interesting to notice how much distance there is between the two interlocutors – as it might tell a lot about how close two people are. Let us imagine that each area is like a bubble that wraps around the person. *"Intimate area"* corresponds to a bubble that covers a distance up to roughly 45 cm – in this area usually only very close people and lovers are allowed without the person feeling uncomfortable. From 45-120 cm is *"personal space"*, reserved for person you are familiar with but not very intimate. 120 cm to 360 cm is classified as *"social space"*, reserved to person you are socially interacting but not familiar: work relationship etc... 360+ cm is *"public space"*, reserved for public events and total strangers. Those bubbles are a reflection of the aura (energetic field generated by the flow of vital energy) of an individual. When you interact with someone else, it is important to observe how the other person reacts and their body language in order to evaluate the proper distance in which the person feels comfortable around you in that given moment. People from different areas might have slightly different comfort zone – according to the environment and culture they come from.

The 3 rules for a great conversation
In order to have a great conversation, it is useful to remember 3 rules:

1) The main topic people like to talk about in conversation is themselves (and anything related like hobbies, work, etc...)
2) Finding commonalities with the other person, and when you can not find one, ask the other person to talk about their work, etc..
3) Conversation works like a multiple layer cake: in order to add a new layer, first add value to the conversation and only at that point you can ask a new question – otherwise the conversation would feel like an interrogatory.

It is also important to think if whatever you are going to say it is true, kind and necessary – if it is, say it and if it is not, avoid saying it.

The Art of Networking
Networking is very powerful – both at personal and business level. Networking can help you have effortless communications and relationships, and it can make a massive difference in obtaining an information or an help that can solve a complicate situation, as well as allowing you to learn a lot of new useful skills (as

every person you meet will be your superior in some ways, and you can learn a lot from that person). An important point to note is – networking must be conducted with a sincere heart, it is not a manipulation technique. A great book to read in this sense is *"How to win friends and influence people"* by Dale Carnegie, great wisdom – here I will quote in nutshell the main techniques:

"IN A NUTSHELL - TECHNIQUES IN HANDLING PEOPLE

Principle 1—Do not criticize, condemn or complain.
Principle 2—Give honest and sincere appreciation.
Principle 3—Arouse in the other person an eager want.

IN A NUTSHELL—SIX WAYS TO MAKE PEOPLE LIKE YOU

Principle 1—Become genuinely interested in other people.
Principle 2—Smile.
Principle 3—Remember that a person's name is to that person the sweetest and most important sound in any language.
Principle 4—Be a good listener. Encourage others to talk about themselves.
Principle 5—Talk in terms of the other person's interests.
Principle 6—Make the other person feel important— and do it sincerely.

IN A NUTSHELL—WIN PEOPLE TO YOUR WAY OF THINKING

Principle 1—The only way to get the best of an argument is to avoid it.

Principle 2—Show respect for the other person's opinions. Never say, "You're wrong."

Principle 3—If you are wrong, admit it quickly and emphatically.

Principle 4—Begin in a friendly way.

Principle 5—Get the other person saying "yes, yes" immediately.

Principle 6—Let the other person do a great deal of the talking.

Principle 7—Let the other person feel that the idea is his or hers.

Principle 8—Try honestly to see things from the other person's point of view.

Principle 9—Be sympathetic with the other person's ideas and desires.

Principle 10—Appeal to the nobler motives.

Principle 11—Dramatize your ideas.

Principle 12—Throw down a challenge.

IN A NUTSHELL—BE A LEADER

A leader's job often includes changing your people's attitudes and behaviours. Some suggestions to accomplish this:

Principle 1— Begin with praise and honest appreciation.

Principle 2—Call attention to people's mistakes indirectly.

Principle 3—Talk about your own mistakes before criticizing the other person.

Principle 4—Ask questions instead of giving direct orders.

Principle 5—Let the other person save his/her face.

Principle 6—Praise the slightest improvement and praise every improvement. Be "hearty in your approbation and lavish in your praise."

Principle 7—Give the other person a fine reputation to live up to.

Principle 8—Use encouragement. Make the fault seems easy to correct.

Principle 9—Make the other person happy about doing the thing you suggest.

IN A NUTSHELL—SEVEN RULES FOR MAKING YOUR HOME LIFE HAPPIER

Rule 1: Don't nag.

Rule 2: Don't try to make your partner over.

Rule 3: Don't criticize.

Rule 4: Give honest appreciation.

Rule 5: Pay little attentions.

Rule 6: Be courteous.

Rule 7: Read a good book on the sexual side of marriage."

For detailed information of each principle, check the book by Dale Carnegie.

How to learn a new language faster

I had the luck of being born with two native languages - Spanish and Italian. Thus I learned as a kid about how to switch from one to the other at will and this makes me easier to learn new languages – which I love to, as it is very fun and a great mind-opener.

We can note 6 scales in the knowledge of a language: A1, A2, B1, B2, C1, C2.

A1 is the lowest level, and C2 is the highest.

Thus A levels can be classified as beginner level, B as intermediate and C as advanced. In order to learn a new language faster, I suggest you to use Assimil method. It's very effective: you start by reading the dialogues in the desired language by confronting them with your native language(s) and periodically there is a lesson about grammar. At half book, you start to translate the dialogues from native to desired language. At the completion of the book, your level would be typically around B2 for standard Assimil books. Keep practicing as much as possible. It is a good idea to buy a detailed syntax book with exercises, to keep it as reference and practice. Read and/or watch film/serial in the desired language, talk with native speakers (a great application to find contacts to help each other practice gratis is GoSpeaky) etc.. At a certain point, you will eventually reach mastery over the language – reaching C1. And the highest is C2: this is a level in which you create a unique style on top of a mastered language. in order to reach this level, you must translate advanced material into the desired language and check the translation to learn new word constructs, read, listen as much as possible in the desired language, you can listen music and sing it, and of course continue practicing with native speakers – and you will eventually reach it. A good way to remember easily words is by using funny mnemonic associations. My father taught me "mnemo" methods as a kid. For example let us say that you want to learn how to say in Spanish butterfly - "mariposa" which can be broken in Italian language as "mare" (sea) plus "posa(re)" – to lay down. So Italians can use easily this funny image: a giant butterfly (with Spanish flag colours) that lays down ("posare" → posa = to lay down) on the sea. ("mari" → mare = sea). You can read more detailed techniques to improve memory in the book "*How to develop a super memory*" by Harry Loraine.

Make your life a drama-free zone

With an increased networking skill, you will also happen to run more often into negative people from time to time. So it is about time to talk about drama and how to prevent and remove it from your life.

Drama does not come by magic in your life. Either you create it with your very hands, or you invite it in your life, or you associate with people who bring it in your life. Therefore, allowing drama or removing it from your life – that is a personal decision. Do not allow haters to tear you down. Haters do not really hate you – in truth they feel very bad about themselves and/or they are jealous of something or a trait you possess and as they feel that you are above them, the only thing they can do is trying to tear you down and bring you down to their level – do not give them a minute of the day.

Judgements are a confession of character and opinions

do not define your reality. What it truly matters is what you think about yourself and to focus on your purpose and goals, taking positive action towards it. The best choice you can make for yourself and for your life is therefore evaluating people by looking at their action and to pick wisely your inner circle. Love yourself first. Love for yourself means that you will not tolerate and enable disrespectful behaviours, drama and people try to put you down. You should therefore remove any toxic people from your life, and only allow in your inner circle friends and lovers that appreciate you, support your growth as individual and who also have a life free from drama.

You should always follow 3 rules:

1) Respect yourself.
2) Respect others
3) Responsibility for your actions.

Inner peace begins in the moment when you choose not to allow other people or events to control your emotions.

Emotion and logic in communication

When a man is communicating with a woman, it is necessary to make some considerations as the basis of reasoning of men and women are usually different (logical based versus emotional based).

When a man talks, the words he says tend to be a more logical representation and purpose driven – so when a man says something, it usually means what he said and it is aimed for a specific practical purpose. Also men usually do not like to talk about problems, but rather prefer to retreat and think on solutions by themselves.

On the other hand everything a woman says and does is about her emotions in the present moment, with a main focus to connection, which sometimes bring a woman to do nasty generalizations etc... Also women usually resolve their problems by talking and sharing their emotions and feelings. Therefore, for an effortless communication between two members of the opposite genders, a mutual effort is needed:

-a man should focus on reading the emotional status and body languages clues that a woman sends, listening her properly (repeating part of what she says and analyse how she feels about it, and asking her to share everything) and putting great emphasis on her emotions and feelings.

-A woman should focus on expressing her emotional needs on a more logical based direction and instructions. A proper way for a man to open up emotionally her woman is as it follows – the man starts by asking how her day was and then let her speak, encouraging her to talk and tell every detail. As she talks, he should repeat some of the part of what she said (to let her know that he is listening) and evaluating what it is happening to her and how it makes her feel. After a while, she will say something on the lines about feeling much better and/or she was glad to have talked with the man – by doing so she will feel relieved and open more and more to the man. When a woman is hurt and/or upset, she might bring up a similar past situation in which she felt the same emotion and/or she will throw hasty generalisation ("you never do this/that.." etc). In these cases, she does not mean to say that "the man never does this/that" as most men will typically assume, but rather than in that moment she feels the man is not doing whatever it is the topic of the conversation. Also a typical way women test men to see if they really care is to say *"I am fine"* when by looking at her it is pretty clear she is not. When that happens, the man should focus on opening her up emotionally, by emphasizing the fact she is not feeling fine and wanting to know what is bothering her – with humour, touch and masculine presence. Eventually she will break down and open up, and by following the same template above mentioned – with a proper apologize on the lines of *"so by doing this, I made you feel like this – and by doing that, I made you feel like that. I should have done like this other way/that other way, so that you felt appreciated. I'm sorry that I hurted you."* and the same relieved response will come and she will fully open up again. In the dating and romantic relationship scene, women love to bluff and test men, either subconsciously and/or consciously, in order to check if the man is centered in his masculine energy and purpose in life. The higher the attraction, the easier the tests will be on the man. The lower the attraction, the more walls she will pull between herself and the man, and the harder her tests will be. A woman knows that if a man truly cares about her, he will show this by actions and not just by words. Also everything a woman does is about being appreciated, so a man should be always appreciative of her woman's effort in her communication and actions (like taking care of her look etc...) - after all a man especially opened her woman up towards himself.

CALMNESS AND THE ART OF NEGOTIATION

Calmness is the most powerful force, giving a person the power to be practically unstoppable. By remaining calm in any situation, you can impartially assess a circumstance, evaluate the best possible solution(s) and take positive action – and this is valid in every area of life, including business and personal relationships.

A great way to calm down is to take deep long breaths as explained in "yin and yang" chapter, when I talked about the relation of mind and body. Everything in life is a negotiation and/or a test that promotes individual growth. Always be prepared. A great preparatory exercise is the yoga technique "*sankalpa*": visualize yourself reaching your aim - like it was in front of your eyes – this will prepare your mind and body at their best – and take positive action. By remaining calm, you can properly evaluate the circumstances and the other views of the other parties on the possible deal for the needed considerations. Assertivity is also an important trait in life: being direct in expressing who you are, what you feel and what you want from a negotiation. Phone should only be used for agreement to meet up, not for giving information. As you are involved in a negotiation, one of the following scenarios can happen:
a) you talk the person/party into getting what you want;
b) the other person/party is not willing to give you what you want, and tries to talk you into getting what they want.

If the two parties views are identical or similar, an agreement will be reached fast. Sometimes negotiation can be longer, with the other party being unsure about the deal. In that case you should do a take away of the offer and consider if it is appropriate to formulate a new counteroffer and if appropriate, you can do at maximum   another try.. However it is important to remember this: *"The strongest negotiating position is being able to walk away and mean it"(Michael Yon).*

If the other party is not willing to give you what you want and you do not want to settle for less of what you want, then you must walk away from the negotiation and mean it. If you are too desperate to conclude a deal, the other party will smell your eagerness to reach an agreement and you will lose any leverage of influence in the negotiation. By walking away, stating your purpose and eventually telling them to get in touch if they reconsider the offer, you are telling them that you value yourself and what you can offer. At that point, either you will reach an agreement with the other party in the future at the desirable terms, or you will conclude a better deal somewhere else at your desired conditions.

DATING AND RELATIONSHIPS

The dating scene changed drastically in the recent period, especially with the introduction of technologies. However the main psychology of sexual polarity between masculine and feminine in dating is always the same. I will do an analysis of how the usual flow goes in a standard situation - considering the case of a man being more centered in his masculine and a woman being more centered in her feminine, which covers at least 90%+ of the usual couples.

Before proceeding, I am going to make two notes:

1) in rare circumstances a woman might enjoy to be more centered in her masculine, and a man to be more centered in his feminine and in that case they can form a sexual polarity between themselves and the frequentation will work great. A woman that enjoys being more in her masculine will found effortless dating a man that enjoys being more in his feminine, and viceversa – otherwise the sexual polarity would not form properly and there are going to be a lot of conflicts – either for leadership (if both are more masculine) or for lack of emotional stability (if both are more feminine).

2) Regarding dating and romantic relationship between two members of the same gender, this flow will be pretty much the same, except that you need to change "man" with the partner being more masculine and "woman" with the partner being more feminine.

Having clarified this, we can proceed with the analysis. In the moment a man and a woman meet for the very first time, either there will be a spark of romantic attraction which can be increased and explored, or there will be not and in that case you should move on and meet someone else. It is just a numbers game, in which some will like you and some will not like you.

Let us assume that the spark of attraction happens and the two have either agreed the details for a first date on the spot or exchanged contact information.

Phone, mail, social networks etc... should be aimed with the purpose to plan definite dates, not for "chatting the whole day". While in long distance relationship it is useful to use phone and/or video-application like Skype to keep periodically in touch, you should always remember the main purpose of using these technologies is to agree on the details for meeting up in person.

Now, two things can happen.

Either the woman has already a high level of attraction to start with, and she will start to chase actively the man from the beginning – like inviting him to meet up etc.. Or alternatively the attraction of the woman is still not high enough for her to chase the man, in which case the man should do a minimal effort by contacting first the woman once for week to plan definite dates - until her attraction becomes high and she will start to chase the man, getting in touch more and more often as her attraction rises and using these occasions in which she contacts him in order to plan a new definite date.

Smart men's mindset on the dating scene is a *"take it or leave it"* attitude (= being happy whatever about being with her or not), not getting attached to the outcome of sex and letting women come and go as they feel comfortable at their own pace. Clueless man will instead seek her approval and try to rush the flow and force situations, which will cause a woman to feel uncomfortable – as she will feel that she might lose her freedom, and also chasing is a feminine trait, thus lowering gradually her attraction (and causing her backing off and testing the man more and more) up to the point of forcing the woman out of their life with their own hands. It is important to remember that in a sexual relationship, an healthy sexual polarity of masculine and feminine is needed or otherwise the attraction will slowly fade. During dates the man should focus on leading the flow of it – logistic details, focusing on her, having fun and in escalating physically as the woman feels ready and gently leading the interaction to the bedroom - while the woman should just focus on showing up, dressing hot, relaxing in her feminine side while following the lead of the man and do most of the talking and connection during the dates. Dates are meant to be an occasion to pass a great time together and enjoy each other, not to be the woman's therapist. Every topic of discussion should be fun and positive, as women will associate emotions they feel around the man with being with that man, also woman should talk most of the time during the date with the man listening properly. Sometimes it might be necessary to talk about a negative topic during dates - in these cases just focus on the positive you gained from the experience and quickly change to a more positive fun topic, reserving more detailed information if necessary, when the dating leads to a more stable relationship. The woman will make extremely clear when she is ready for every step of a physical escalation and layers of frequentation – so the man should pay attention on her and her body language.

Good rules about physical escalation are:

1) *touching a woman is appropriate when she issues an invitation (with non-verbal signals of attraction like bumping into the man or if she consciously initiate to touch themselves) and touch should be kept as long as the woman does not withdraw from touching – waiting the next invitation to touch again from the woman, it is a way women use to subtly test if a man pursues her more than she pursues him – and as previously said, chasing is a feminine trait so over-pursuing by the man part would cause rejection on long term.*

2) *When she is ready to be kissed, she will send clear non-verbal clues (check back the body languages tips in which I mentioned about woman's non-verbal attraction clues). Sometimes she might even kiss by first intention in case of high attraction and direct personality, but usually a woman will rarely do the first move.*

3) *Kissing eventually bring the situation to the point of making out heavily, which lead in turn to the man suggesting the woman to go somewhere else more private (like his or her place) to drink something together. In that private location, with a two steps forward and one step backwards mentality, the man*

gradually escalates physically as she is receptive and open to it, and by continuing to build rapport if she temporarily steps back in the escalation, so that when the women feels fully ready - they hook up.

On average most women will sleep with a man by the 2nd or 3rd date – the process can become faster if a date is planned to flow in 2/3 different places, thus giving the feeling of multiple dates at once to the woman. Usually after a few dates, the woman will reach out in less then a week as her attraction grows, thus she starts to chase actively the man and at this point the man should just sit back and use these opportunities to plan definite dates. During the first two months of a frequentation, a woman will do a specific test - disappearing for a week, even if everything is great.

It is just a way to check if the man is needy (thus potentially risking to lose her freedom, and in the worst case scenario of him becoming a stalker) or if he is strong and centered in his masculine and purpose in life – the correct way to pass this test is to ask how she feels the next week without making drama about her behaviour. A woman will always test a man when she is attracted romantically – by bluffing and doing different kind of tests, whatever they are subconsciously or consciously, to check if the man is centered on his masculine energy. As the attraction of a woman rise, these tests will become easier and easier to pass – as the attraction lowers, she will back off more and test him more with harder tests. By doing everything correctly, typically in at least 2+ months of dating the woman will pretty much contact at least once daily the man and bring up the topic of being in love with him, and wanting to be exclusive as the man became her emotional mountain. The man must be the mountain and the leader of the relationship, so that the woman can be playful and relaxed in her feminine side. According to the wishes of both, at that point if the frequentation continues - either it becomes an exclusive relationship or it is kept as a casual open relationship. True love is freedom. The purpose of any kind of relationship is to give, wanting the other person to be happy and helping the other person to grow in a better version of themself. In exclusive relationships most men do two fatal mistakes: one being that they stop being appreciative and courting the woman properly, and the second is that they do not know how to communicate properly with their woman and opening her up back to her feminine side – thus causing her to shift more and more to her masculine side with the result that the polarity starts to slowly dissipate. It is easy to see when that happens: usually these couples wear the same exact dresses, the woman stops taking care of her look (hair, nails,..), she starts to lead the relationship instead of her man and you can even spot in her face the fact she is being resentful for the weakness of her man, as they become colder and more distant towards each other. At that point it is only a matter of time until a breakup happens or they just stay together for the kids (but the passion is completely gone). A woman who is satisfied of her romantic relationship takes a great care of her look, tends to grow her hair longer and she might colour nails etc.. and you can see her being relaxed and playful in the company of her man as she follows his lead.

It is important to remember that courtship never ends, and the points I made about communication between emotional and logical mind. Sometimes a relationship might run its course even by doing everything correctly by both parts, due to external life-changing circumstances that bring a relationship to be in extremely difficult conditions to continue - and if the decision is mutual, with both people involved being mature people and great communicators, you should take a period of break to sort all the mixed feelings and after that by all means you can remain friends: it is the most loving way to close a relationship in this kind of scenario. In the case of a breakup which is not a mutual decision, the strongest negotiating position for the dumped is to do not agree to be friends only, stating to be interested just in romance and to get in touch in the case of a change of heart of the dumper, then walk away and mean it – at that point if you are the dumped, the dumper must do 100% of the chasing to make up for the breakup. If you are the dumper and you realized that you made a mistake, you can contact the dumped once apologizing for your behaviour and asking for a definite date – if everything goes well, the courtship flow returns to be normal and if the dumped says no to meet up, tell the dumped to contact you in the future in case of changing idea, then walk away and never look back. People either grow together or they grow alone. Marriage is not a pre-requisite for a great romantic relationship and it should be evaluated carefully by the couple, and if this option is chosen - it should be because of love.

THE STRATEGICAL WISDOM OF SUN TZU

A popular saying is *"In love and in war everything is allowed"*. Sun Tzu was a war strategist, to the point of writing a book known as "The Art of War". Even though life is a journey and not a competition, knowing the main principles of warfare can be quite useful in several occasions (sport, competitions, self-defense, etc...). In a nutshell, these are the 36 main stratagems in the art of warfare.

FOR COMMANDING SUPERIORITY

1) **Deceive the heavens and cross the ocean:** mask your real goals with a fake one, until your aims are achieved – the constant false alarms will annoy so much the enemy that they will lower their guard when you make your real move.

2) **Beseige Wei to rescue Zhao:** instead of a head-on battle with a strong enemy, avoid it and strike at his weakness (like a weaker ally)

3) **Kill with a borrowed knife:** causing damage to an enemy party by getting a third party to do the damage or by causing a civil war.

4) **Substitute leisure for labour:** have your troops be fresh and prepared for battle, while your enemy is rushing to fight against you – ideally resulting in an exhausted enemy troops running into your fresh soldier in the terms of your choosing.

5) **Loot a burning house:** the best time to attack

an opponent is when they have their own problems to deal with and their focus is disrupted. However you should be careful to not become trapped in the burning house as well.

6) ***Clamour in the East, attack in the West:*** *get the enemy to focus his forces elsewhere, then proceed to attack a position that would be weakly defended. Deception and factor of surprise are crucial game-changers in a war.*

FOR CONFRONTATION

7) ***Create something from nothing:*** *Make somebody believes there was something when there is in fact nothing, or vice versa. Having fallen for a trick one or two times – the enemy will be not willing to fall for a third time for a trick – and that is when you should actually attack.*

8) ***Openly repair the walkway, but sneak through the passage of Chencang:*** *deceive the opponent with an obvious approach that will take an extended period of time or a deception ploy, while surprising him by taking a shortcut to sneak up on him or to conceal another ploy from their attention.*

9) ***Observe the fire from the opposite shore, or sit on the mountain and watch the tigers fight:*** *the ideal moment to enter the battlefield is when all other players have become exhausted, fighting amongst themselves, to go in at full strength*

and pick up the pieces.

10) **Hide a knife behind a smile:** *Charm and ingratiate yourself to your enemy, and once you gained his trust, move against him in secret.*

11) **Sacrifice the Plum Tree to preserve the Peach Tree:** *Sacrifice short-term objectives in order to reach the long-term goal.*

12) **Take the opportunity to pilfer a goat:** *While carrying your plans, be flexible enough in order to take advantage on any possible opportunity – no matter how small, slight, profit you can get from it.*

FOR ATTACKING

13) **Beat the grass to startle the snake:** *do something without aim, but make it extremely spectacular to provoke a response of the opponent – making him giving away his plans and/or position; or just taunt him. Do something unusual, weird, and unexpected as this will arouse the enemy's suspicion and disrupt his thinking. However be careful – an imprudent act might give your position or intentions away to the the opponent.*

14) **Borrow a corpse to resurrect the soul:** *Revive something from the past and give it a new purpose or remodel it to your advantage.*

15) **Lure the tiger down from the mountain:** *Lure your enemy away from his field of advantage, in this way you will separate him*

from his source of strength.

16) **To catch something, first set it free:** *a cornered prey will often try a final desperation attack – to prevent it, let the enemy believes that he still has a chance for freedom.*

17) **Toss out a brick to attract Jade:** *Lure someone by making him believe he gains something or to just make him react to it and to obtain something valuable from him in return.*

18) **To capture the bandits, capture their leader:** *if an opponent army is strong, but he follows his leadership only for money or threat – take aim at the leader, and the rest of the army will disperse or come over to your side. If they are allied to their leader by loyalty, beware that the army can continue to fight on after his death out of vengeance.*

FOR CONFUSED SITUATIONS

19) **Steal the firewood from under the pot:** *Take out the leading argument(s) and/or asset(s) of your opponent, in order to deny your enemy the leverage and resources needed to fight you.*

20) **Stir up the waters to catch a fish:** *Create confusion, and use this confusion to lower the opponent guard and further your own goals.*

21) **Slough off the cicada's golden shell:** *create an illusion to fit your aims and goals, and to distract others.*

22) **Shut the door to catch the thief:** *If you have*

the possibility to completely catch the enemy then you should do so, thereby bringing the battle or war to a quick and lasting end.

23) **Befriend a distant state while attacking a neighbour:** *When you are the strongest in the battlefield, your greatest threat is from the second strongest in your field, not the strongest from another field, and thus the distant neighbour will make a good ally, however temporary.*

24) **Obtain safe passage to conquer the state of Guo:** *Borrow the resources of an ally to attack a common enemy. Once the opponent is beaten, use those resources to turn on the ally that lent you them in the first place.*

FOR GAINING GROUND

25) **Replace the beams with rotten timbers:** *Disrupt the opponent's formations, interfere with their methods of operations, change the rules which they are used to follow, go contrary to their standard training.*

26) **Point at the mulberry tree, but curse the locust:** *To discipline, control, or warn others whose status or position excludes them from a direct confrontation, you should use analogy and innuendo. without directly calling names: those accused cannot retaliate without revealing their complicity.*

27) **Feign madness but keep your balance:** *Hide behind the mask of a fool, a drunk, or a madman to create confusion about your true*

intentions and motivations.

28) **Lure them onto the roof, then take away the ladder:** *With baits and deceptions, lure your enemy into a treacherous terrain, then proceed to cut off his lines of communication and avenue of escape; to save himself, he must fight not only your own army but also the elements of nature.*

29) **Deck the tree with false blossoms:** *Through the use of deception, artifice and disguise, make something of no value appear valuable; of no threat appear dangerous; of no use appear useful.*

30) **Exchange the roles of host and guest:** *Usurp leadership in a situation where you are normally a subordinate. Infiltrate your target by pretending to be a guest to be accepted, and then develop from inside and become the ruler later.*

FOR DESPERATE STRAITS

31) **The Beauty Trap:** *Send your enemy beautiful women to cause discord within his camp. First, the ruler becomes so in love with the beauty that he starts to neglect his duties and allows his guard to lower; second, other males at court will begin to display aggressive behaviours that inflames minor differences hindering co-operation and destroying morale in the army; third, other females at court, motivated by jealousy and envy, begin to plot*

intrigues, further creating chaos and exacerbating the situation.

32) **The Empty Fort Strategy:** *When the opponent is superior in numbers and your situation is such that you can make an educated guess to be overrun at any moment, then drop all pretense of military preparedness and act calmly so that the enemy will think you have hidden reserves and want to trap them into the fort.*

33) **Let the enemy's own spy sow discord in the enemy camp:** *Undermine your enemy's intelligence-gathering abilities by using his own spies against him or planting your own agents among his.*

34) **Injure yourself to gain the enemy's trust:** *pretending to be injured has two possible applications. In the first, the enemy is lulled into relaxing his guard since he no longer considers you to be an immediate threat. The second is a way of ingratiating yourself to your enemy by pretending the injury was caused by a mutual enemy.*

35) **Chain stratagems:** *In important matters, one should use several stratagems applied simultaneously after another as in a chain of stratagems. Keep different plans operating in an overall scheme; however, in this manner if any one strategy fails, then the chain breaks and the whole scheme fails.*

36) **If all else fails, retreat:** *The best battle is one fought with your side never having to*

mobilize, but if it becomes obvious that your current course of action will lead to defeat, then retreat and regroup.

Knowing these principles can be useful in various situations, so you should calmly and impartially assess the circumstances and evaluate how to properly take action. In *"The Art of War"* of Sun Tzu you can find a more detailed strategical analysis of the art of warfare.

If you know the enemy and know yourself, you need not fear the result of a hundred battles.

- Sun Tzu

<u>HOW TO DEAL WITH HARD SITUATIONS</u>

Life sometimes can be pretty hard.

For example, I will tell you about something my grandfather Domenico, who passed away many years ago. Among the several difficulties he faced - his father died when he was 11 years old and he had immediately to start working as a kid for the sake of his family, he was involved in WW2 as a soldier on the battlefield for 5 years just after marrying and he had to fight in treacherous terrains - almost froze his feet in winter and he had to be hospitalized for a month before returning home. Despite everything he had to pass, he never broke down and he lived a good life.

In my life, I had to pass 7 hard months in which I lost my 3 remaining grandparents (my Spanish grandmother died instead when I was a kid), one after the another – and it was pretty hard. When I passed such a hard moment, there was a story that helped me.

"There once lived a king in an eastern land – the king was extremely moody and he was constantly torn between being generous with the population to periods of extreme despotism. The smallest things could make him suddenly really upset or making him overreact emotionally. One day the king got tired of the situation, and started to seek a way out. He asked a wise man, reputed for his wisdom, for help in order to find balance, peace and serenity in his life – offering him whatever he wanted in exchange. The wise man replied that the price for it would have been too much high, even for the whole kingdom, so he would have given him the solution as a gift at the condition that he

had honoured it. The king agreed, and the wise man returned a few weeks later. He gifted the king with a box, in which there was a ring. The king was surprised, and in the ring he noticed a simple inscription carved on it: "This too shall pass". The wise man replied to him by saying that the king should always wear this ring, and no matter what happens – before labelling the situation good or bad, touch the ring and read the inscription in it – in this way, peace will be always with you."

In yoga, we can express "titiksa" with a phrase:
"pain is inevitable, but suffering is optional".
Inner peace begins in the moment in which you do not let other people or events to control your emotions.
Life is a flow, stagnation is death.
People come and go in your life.
Situations and circumstances change.
Attaching to how things were and overthinking are the roots of all suffering – the only real moment is the "here and now". Yoga is a way to freedom – by practicing it, you learn how to meditate and by doing so to free yourself from negative feelings, fear and suffering.
Speaking of a meditation, one of the branches of yoga is Tantra, which is often misunderstood in the western.
Tantra is much more than sexual techniques – which they are a part of it. Sex feels great not only for biological reasons, but also because it is a form of meditation and tantra deeply explores that aspect.
It goes into great detail on how to use sex as a form of advanced combined meditation with masculine

energy's freedom being about breaking barriers and please the partner, and feminine energy's freedom being about love and connection to the partner. Sexual techniques are just one of the aspect of Tantra, but not the main aim of it.

Returning to hard situations, they are merely meant for education purposes and for strengthening and make you wiser. If you look at archery, in order to shoot an arrow, you must place the arrow on the bow, pull the arrow backwards and when it is ready for maximum shot power – aim at the target, you let it go and fire it. In the same way when life is "pulling you backwards" with difficulties, it actually means that you are about to be launched into something greater, so take the needed time to grief – but then stand up, just focus, remain positive and keep aiming to your goals and dreams.

As a final note, if you have not already achieved it, one day you will reach a point in which you are truly at peace and in touch with yourself, nothing anyone says or does bothers you anymore, negativity and drama can no longer affect you. That point is called in zen practice as "zen point" and the event that triggers the reaching of this point will be unique to each person. After all, everyone's life journey is different.

FINAL CONSIDERATIONS

Our walk together in this book ends here.
I suggest you to read again the book from time to time, and to use any possible occasion to put in practice what you learned – until the knowledge of this book will be instinctive to you. If you find yoga interesting, a great book to start your own personal practice is *"I learn yoga"* by Andre Van Lysebeth.

If you appreciated this book, you are welcome to suggest it to all your family and dear ones, as well as to like my facebook page: facebook.com/theinteriorlight
If you need a personal life coaching help (especially in yoga, dating or negotiation skills) and you are serious about being coached, then you can email me at theinteriorlight@gmail.com (maximum message size 2-3 paragraphs), and I will gladly reply to you when I have free time and it is more convenient to me.

That said, once the assimilation is fully completed by reading and putting in practice the techniques of this book, your greatness will be fully activated. You will be fully in control of yourself and of your life, smiling more, spreading more positive energy, kindness and love in this universe. You became the light.

NAMASTE
I honor the place in you where the entire Universe resides. I honor the light, love, truth, beauty and peace within you, because it is also within me.
In sharing these things we are united, we are the same, we are one.